LIGHTNING BOLT BOOKS™

What's on My Plate?
Choosing from the Five Food Groups

Jennifer Boothroyd

Lerner Publications • Minneapolis

For Claire and Gavin

Lerner Publications Company
A division of Lerner Publishing Group, Inc.
241 First Avenue North
Minneapolis, MN 55401 USA

For reading levels and more information, look up this title at www.lernerbooks.com.

Library of Congress Cataloging-in-Publication Data

Boothroyd, Jennifer, 1972– author.
    What's on my plate? / Jennifer Boothroyd.
        pages cm. — (Lightning bolt books™. Healthy eating)
    Audience: Ages 5–8.
    Audience: K to grade 3.
    Includes bibliographical references and index.
    ISBN 978-1-4677-9470-1 (lb : alk. paper) — ISBN 978-1-4677-9671-2 (pb : alk. paper) — ISBN 978-1-4677-9672-9 (eb pdf)
    1. Nutrition—Juvenile literature. 2. Food—Juvenile literature. 3. Diet—Juvenile literature. I. Title. II. Title: What is on my plate?
RA784.B6372 2016
613.2—dc23   2015020567

Manufactured in the United States of America
2-42815-20524-8/15/2016

Table of Contents

We Need Food

Time to eat! Food gives our bodies energy.

What is your favorite meal?

Food also gives our bodies nutrients. Nutrients help us stay healthy.

Different foods have different nutrients.

There are five main food groups. We should eat foods from each group every day.

Each of these foods is from one of the five food groups.

Fruits and Vegetables

Fruits and vegetables are two important food groups. They are a large part of a healthy diet.

What fruits and veggies do you like?

Fruits make a yummy cereal topping.

Bananas and blueberries are fruits. Many fruits taste sweet.

8

Kids your age should eat about 1 to 1.5 cups (150 to 225 grams) of fruit every day. That's at least thirty-two grapes or one large banana.

The vegetables in this salad are raw.

Broccoli and peas are vegetables. Some people like to eat cooked vegetables. Some people eat them raw.

You should eat about 1.5 cups (225 g) of vegetables each day. **Eighteen baby carrots or three stalks of celery are the right amount.**

It is important to eat different types of vegetables. Vegetables can make your meal colorful too.

Grains

Grains are plants like wheat, oats, and rice. Many types of bread are made from grains.

Some grains are called whole grains. Whole grains have more nutrients than refined grains.

Refined grains have been milled, or ground up. Milling removes some of a grain's nutrients.

Brown rice and oatmeal are whole grains. White rice and plain bagels are made from refined grains.

Whole grain cereal makes a healthy breakfast.

Try to choose a cereal without much sugar.

You should eat about 5 ounces (142 g) of grain foods each day. Half should be whole grains. Eating 1 cup (28 g) of corn flakes cereal, 1 cup (140 g) of whole wheat noodles, and a small tortilla is enough grains for a day.

Proteins and Dairy

Meat and eggs have lots of protein. Our bodies use protein to grow muscles.

Eating an omelet can help build muscles!

Grilled chicken has little fat. Too much fat can be bad for your heart.

Chicken and fish are good meats to eat. They often have less fat than other types of meat. That makes them healthy choices.

Not all protein comes from animals. Nuts and beans also have protein.

Nuts are a tasty and crunchy protein source.

Four ounces (113 g) of high-protein foods is what you need each day. You can get 1 ounce (28 g) of protein from twelve almonds or one egg.

This egg-and-veggie sandwich makes a healthy lunch.

Many dairy foods come from cows.

Dairy foods have calcium. Calcium makes bones grow strong.

Skim milk has no fat and lots of nutrients.

Milk is a dairy food. It is used to make yogurt and cheese. Choose dairy foods carefully. Some of these foods have too much fat.

Your body needs 2.5 cups (591 milliliters) of dairy every day.

Sometimes Foods

Some foods are not very healthy. These foods have few nutrients.

They also might have too much sugar. Candy and soda have lots of sugar. Too much sugar is bad for our teeth.

These candies are full of sugar.

Other foods have too much
fat. French fries and ice
cream can have lots of fat.

Cake is a sometimes food.

These are foods we should eat only sometimes.

People need to make good choices to have a healthy diet.

Eating a healthy diet gives you energy to work and play!

Try This!

Are you eating enough of all five food groups? A good way to check is to keep a food log. Write down everything you eat during a day. Make sure you write how much you ate too. After a few days, take a look at how you did. Did you get enough of each food group each day? Are you eating too much of certain groups? Talk to an adult about what you could do to eat a healthier diet.

Fun Facts

- Some foods we eat are made from more than one food group. A stir-fry, tacos, and lasagna can have vegetables, protein, grains, and dairy.

- When your family grocery shops, spend more time near the walls of the store. Most stores keep fruits and veggies in the outside aisles.

- Dairy foods have lots of calcium, but so do leafy green veggies such as broccoli and kale. These veggies are a great way to get calcium if you don't or can't drink milk.

Glossary

calcium: a mineral found in some foods. It helps bones and teeth.

diet: the foods and drinks you usually consume

fat: an oily substance in foods

nutrient: something needed by plants and animals to live and grow

protein: a substance in meat and some plants

raw: uncooked

refined: a grain that has had some parts removed to change its texture. Refined grains do not have as many nutrients as whole grains.

Further Reading

Bellisario, Gina. *Choose Good Food! My Eating Tips.* Minneapolis: Millbrook Press, 2014.

Cleary, Brian P. *Apples, Cherries, Red Raspberries: What Is in the Fruits Group?* Minneapolis: Millbrook Press, 2011.

Go, Slow, and Whoa! A Kid's Guide to Eating Right
http://kidshealth.org/kid/stay_healthy/food/go_slow_whoa.html

Kreisman, Rachelle. *You Want Me to Eat That? A Kids' Guide to Eating Right.* Egremont, MA: Red Chair, 2015.

MyPlate Kids' Place
http://www.choosemyplate.gov/kids

Index

Photo Acknowledgments

The images in this book are used with the permission of: © Nata-Lia/Shutterstock.com, p. 2; © Mark Bowden/Vetta/Getty Images, p. 4; © Jacek Chabreszewski/Shutterstock .com, p. 5; © Hurst Photo/Shutterstock.com, p. 6; © RTimages/Shutterstock.com, p. 7; © Kim Nguyen/Shutterstock.com, p. 8; © Rekha Garton/Getty Images, p. 9; © Darryl Brooks/Shutterstock.com, p. 10; © Denis Vrublevski/Shutterstock.com, p. 11; © elena Schweitzer/Shutterstock.com, p. 12; © Zurbagan/Shutterstock.com, p. 13; © ERproductions Ltd/Blend Images/Getty Images, p. 14; © Hero Images/Getty Images, p. 15; © HandmadePictures/Shutterstock.com, p. 16; © Vankad/Shutterstock.com, p. 17; © Cefo design/Shutterstock.com, p. 18; © Hermina/Shutterstock.com, p. 19; © Arctic Images/Alamy, p. 20; © JGI/Jamie Grill/Blend Images/Getty Images, p. 21; © Tetra Images/Getty Images, p. 22; © Timolina/Shutterstock.com, p. 23; © OlegDoroshin /Shutterstock.com, p. 24; © Dmitry_T/Shutterstock.com, p. 25; © Ryan McVay/Getty Images, p. 26; © Jupiterimages/Getty Images, p. 27; © Maximilian Stock Ltd. /Photolibrary/Getty Images, p. 28; © Tischenko Irina/Shutterstock.com, p. 30.

Front cover: © iStockphoto.com/YinYang (plate, fruits, vegetables, grains, and milk); © Viktor1/Shutterstock.com (sliced chicken); © AS Food studio/Shutterstock.com (grilled pork).

Main body text set in Johann Light 30/36.